CLOISTER

BOOKS

Cloister Books are inspired by the monastic custom of walking slowly and reading or meditating in the monastery cloister, a place of silence, centering, and calm. Within these pages you will find a similar space in which to pray and reflect on the presence of God.

Going Home

Going Home

AN INVITATION TO JUBILEE

Frank T. Griswold

COWLEY PUBLICATIONS
Cambridge · Boston
Massachusetts

BV
4509.5
. G695
2001

Library of Congress Cataloging-in-Publication Data:
Griswold, Frank T., 1937–
    Going Home : an invitation to jubilee / Frank T. Griswold.
    p. cm. — (Cloister Books)
    ISBN 1-56101-186-X (alk. paper)
    1. Christian life. 2. Jubilee (Judaism) I. Title. II. Series.
BV4509.5 .G695 2001
263—dc21   00-064520

Scripture quotations are taken from *The New Revised Standard Version* of the Bible, © 1989, by the Division of Christian Education of the National Council of the Churches of Christ in the United States of America. Used by permission.

Vicki Black, editor and designer
Cover art: Wheatfield in wool stitchery with appliquéd net, designed and worked by Mrs. E. J. Thomson
Author photo: ENS / Jim Solheim

This book was printed by Versa Press in the United States of America on recycled, acid-free paper.

Cowley Publications
28 Temple Place • Boston, Massachusetts 02111
800-225-1534 • www.cowley.org

Because I believe that preaching is, at its heart, a dialog, I am deeply grateful to those who worshiped together daily at the 73rd General Convention of the Episcopal Church, and thus drew forth these reflections from me.

This book is dedicated in thanksgiving for all those who have lived and shared the gospel with me over the years, and shown me the face of Christ.

◊

Contents

Foreword

This book first took shape as a series of meditations for the morning eucharists during the General Convention of the Episcopal Church in the summer of 2000. Cowley Publications has wisely decided that the spiritual wisdom of Presiding Bishop Frank T. Griswold should have a wider audience. We all need to hear his message that it is the human heart, not some dictum from "the church," that begins the process of jubilee, as "we find ourselves stretched and cracked open by God's own joy and desire for our full flourishing."

I first met Frank Griswold during my seminary years when he led an unforgettable prayer workshop on Ignatian meditation. He continues to be an inspiring teacher. These jubilee meditations, pondered and savored, can help our hearts stretch and crack open to God and, in the author's words, beckon us home to our "belovedness." Read these pages slowly in the style of *lectio divina* ("holy reading"), leaving time for reflection and attentive listening to the Spirit—between paragraphs, sentences, and even individual words.

The moment when 1999 slipped into 2000 gave pundits and prophets an opportunity to assess the past, present, and future condition of the world. In a similar way, jubilee helps both the church and her individual members to focus their attention on an even more specific question: how are we responding to the call of the Jesus Christ who was born, who died, and who rose again two millennia ago?

The idea of jubilee had its roots many years before Jesus' birth in the book of Leviticus: "You shall hallow the fiftieth year and you shall proclaim liberty throughout the land to all its inhabitants"—although there is no evidence that it actually took place. But Frank Griswold shows us that it can take place now. This time is a "season of unfoldment in which God's blessing, compassion, and justice are unleashed, not from some remote heaven but from within the human heart."

What better description of the Christian journey could there be? Being stretched and cracked open by God's own joy and desire for our full flourishing leads us to acknowledge that it is not only ourselves who need to flourish: we, as the body of Christ in the world, are called to be agents of healing for the entire earth. We are, in Griswold's words, to be "caught up in the work of repair."

The concept of jubilee has its roots in the idea of sabbath—a time of "re-creation, reordering, and release." We discover that sabbath first in our own prayer, as our hearts are re-created, reordered, and released from those things which bind us. Such prayer will begin the slow process of transformation in our hearts, helping to free us from the need to dominate the world around us, and thereby freeing others, and the land itself, from the evil consequences of our domination.

In Leviticus, the land was to be granted a sabbath: it was to be plowed but not sown. Today, jubilee gives us a new opportunity to forge a

Christian response to the environmental crisis. Considering honestly and prayerfully the consequences of our domination of nature is likely to lead us to what Griswold calls "a radical shift in how and what we see." Freed from our old patterns of thought, we can begin to live according to a new vision of our place in the great web of life imagined by an ingenious Creator. Then, not only are we less likely to do further harm, but we can learn ways to contribute to nature's healing.

God's sabbath peace, or *shalom*, involves our material wealth as well. Leviticus envisioned an economic reshuffling that equalized the disparities between the rich and the poor. As our hearts are cracked open to our own belovedness, we inevitably grow in compassion. God's transforming grace helps our competitiveness give way to a desire for community and a sense of solidarity with the poor.

Israel's jubilee year was to be a time for the release of captives and the freeing of slaves. Ours is a time to look truthfully at those things which enslave both ourselves and our neighbors around the world. Like the monks of St. Benedict, we can "listen...with the ear of the heart," and learn to hear as God hears and see as God sees, releasing the fear and prejudice that separate us one from another.

The jubilee vision born of the belovedness we experience in our prayer will nurture reconciliation and respect for the world and the people around us. But the vision will be merely a beginning, for it is the ongoing work of a lifetime to learn to live the jubilee life modeled by Jesus Christ.

The many ways this life will be incarnated in our lives will be as various as we ourselves are different one from the other. This valuable book will guide and teach us as we explore for ourselves what jubilee means. In the process, we will not only discover *shalom* within our spirits, but be bearers of that *shalom* to the earth and all her creatures in response to the Risen One's call to us: "You are gifted with my grace, you are the light of the world. Now go forth in my name, proclaim jubilee, and above all, surprise me."

Nancy Roth

Preface

This book is not intended to be read through at a rapid pace. I hope that you might see it as an invitation to reflection. I offer these few suggestions as to how it might be used either privately or with others.

Read slowly with an eye on insight rather than the acquisition of information. Where does the text engage my spirit? Stop there and ask the Spirit of Truth, the Spirit of Christ at work in your consciousness to draw you deeper, possibly beyond the words themselves into a place of insight which reveals a personal invitation.

Pay attention when you feel unsettled or challenged. The Spirit can speak to us there, too.

Ask yourself: How am I being invited to incarnate and live jubilee? How are we as a church, a congregation, a diocese being called to be persons or communities of jubilee? What concrete steps do I need to take, do we need to take, to share Christ's "jubilee consciousness"? Such questions require self-examination and repentance: a change of heart and a change of direction. They therefore challenge us at the deepest levels and expose patterns of resistance and self-preservation which are not easy to face. Yet they, too, are invitations from Christ to enter into the freedom promised to those who make their home in Christ's word.

Remember always that God is a God of compassion and encouragement rather than of judgment.

It is my hope and prayer that these reflections will serve to strengthen and encourage you as you seek, in fellowship with others, to live the mystery of Christ in us: the hope of glory "yet to be revealed."

one

The Year of the Lord's Favor

The spirit of the Lord GOD is upon me, because the LORD has anointed me; he has sent me to bring good news to the oppressed, to bind up the brokenhearted, to proclaim liberty to the captives, and release to the prisoners; to proclaim the year of the LORD's favor, and the day of vengeance of our God; to comfort all who mourn; to provide for those who mourn in

Zion—to give them a garland instead of ashes, the oil of gladness instead of mourning, the mantle of praise instead of a faint spirit. They will be called oaks of righteousness, the planting of the LORD, *to display his glory. They shall build up the ancient ruins, they shall raise up the former devastations; they shall repair the ruined cities, the devastations of many generations.*

Isaiah 61:1-4

2

The spirit of the Lord GOD is upon me," says the prophet. "He has sent me to bring good news to the oppressed . . . to proclaim the year"—not just any year but *the* year—"of the LORD's favor." The same Spirit is lavished upon us in our baptism when we are sealed by the Spirit and marked as Christ's own forever.

And the same vocation is given to us: to bring good news of God in Christ, in word and deed and the example of our lives, to men and women who are bound and oppressed and cut off from the glorious freedom and abundant life God intends for all through the life, death, and resurrection of Christ.

Such is the nature of the year of the Lord's favor, a season we dare to claim in which God— in the full force of God's unrelenting love—seeks to embrace, bless, and reorder the structures of our lives and relationships so they become transparent. So they reveal the way in which God looks upon us and all creation—the creation which surrounds and sustains us and of which we are a part in virtue of our having been formed from the earth.

The year of the Lord's favor is a season of unfoldment in which God's blessing, compassion, and justice are unleashed, not from some remote heaven but from within the human heart—from within our own hearts—as we find ourselves stretched and cracked open by God's own joy and desire for our full flourishing. This flourishing includes not only us, but all others who are held captive by structures and systems, and by patterns of thought and self-perception that work against God's intent and desire.

Let us be reminded here that God's justice is larger and more expansive than our human concept of justice. Our concept is often reduced to what is considered fair by one group or another. In scripture, particularly in the psalms, God's justice is equated with God's righteousness:

4

> Give the King your justice, O God,
>   and your righteousness to the
>   King's Son;
> That he may rule your people righteously
>   and the poor with justice;
> That the mountains may bring prosperity
>   to the people,
>   and the little hills bring righteousness.
> He shall defend the needy among the
>   people;
>   he shall rescue the poor and crush the
>   oppressor. (Psalm 72:1-4)

God's justice and righteousness consist of the ordering of all things according to God's imagination and desire. All things are conformed to God's way of seeing and acting toward and in this world.

The Year of the Lord's Favor

What is justice then? It is to see as God sees and to act as God acts. Justice requires of us a transformation of consciousness, a conformation to the mind of Christ, worked into us over time by the Holy Spirit who draws from what is Christ's and weaves it into the fabric of our lives personally and as a community of faith. This is not easy to grasp or to take into ourselves, but isn't this what we are about as Christians, as the body of Christ in the world? As we move through our days, are we mindful that we run the risk of transformation? Are we aware that we are being conformed, day by day, to the mind of Christ? We are called to be the servants of God's favor for the sake of one another and our world. Together, as best we can, we are responding to that call.

The year of the Lord's favor has another and very specific meaning: it is the jubilee year described in the book of Leviticus.

> You shall hallow the fiftieth year and you shall proclaim liberty throughout the land to all its inhabitants. It shall be a jubilee for you: you shall return, every one of you, to your property and every one of you to your family. That fiftieth year shall be a

jubilee for you: you shall not sow, or reap the aftergrowth, or harvest the unpruned vines. For it is a jubilee; it shall be holy to you: you shall eat only what the field itself produces. (Leviticus 25:10-12)

6   The jubilee year has its roots in the notion of sabbath, which is understood not simply as a day of rest but as a time of re-creation, reordering, and release. All members of a household are released from productive work, along with the ox and donkey and other livestock. Release is also extended to those outside the community, to the resident alien within the town.

On the sabbath, humankind as well as animals share in what the late Rabbi Abraham Joshua Heschel described as an armistice. He writes: "The seventh day is an armistice in man's cruel struggle for existence, a truce in all conflicts personal and social, peace between man and man, man and nature, peace within." He then goes further: "Sabbath is more than an armistice, more than an interlude; it is a profound conscious harmony of man and the world, a sympathy for all things and a participation in the spirit that unites what is below into what is above."[1]

Shabat shalom—sabbath peace. This traditional sabbath greeting is all embracing, all transforming, all reconciling: it changes our hearts of stone into hearts of flesh and makes us capable of expressing mutuality and justness. It makes us able to see as God sees—with unbounded compassion and a love that burns within us for the whole creation. In the midst of life-denying circumstances, this deep peace makes it possible for us to remain steadfast, reflecting and revealing God's hopeful imagination.

The sabbath, extended into a sabbatical or seventh year, then became a jubilee year: seven times seven plus one—thereby representing fullness and completion, with fifty indicating a new beginning, the dawn of a new era.

Though never really achieved in the history of Israel, the jubilee year represents for them, as it does for us at this very moment, a hope, a yearning, a desire, an invitation to enter more fully into God's project and to live in communion with the divine compassion as active agents of God's *shalom,* God's transforming peace.

Were we able to become persons who embody jubilee, we would find ourselves caught up into the work of repair. Those who embrace the year of the Lord's favor, we are told, "shall repair the ruined cities" (Isaiah 61:4). And elsewhere in Isaiah we hear that one who lives as a person of compassion will be called a "repairer of the breach" and "restorer of the streets." This notion of repair gave rise in Jewish tradition to the understanding of sabbath and jubilee as *tikkum olam*: repair of the world. In this spirit, all who share the blessing of Jubilee are called to become actively involved.

We cannot, however, enter into the work of repair, of building up, of rebuilding, easily or lightly. We ourselves must undergo repair, not on our own terms but on God's terms, both personally and corporately, not once but again and again.

At my investiture as Presiding Bishop in the Washington Cathedral, I referred to the words Christ spoke to St. Francis from the cross: "Go rebuild my church." These words apply to us all in every age. To undergo repair, to be rebuilt—both personally and as a church, is costly and profoundly unsettling. It shatters and pierces our false sense of peace that allows us to reject or limit God's justness and righteousness. It obliges us to be stripped of our illusions, our narrow and self-serving views. It involves the cross, our dying in order to enter into the new creation, the new consciousness that enables us, in union with Christ, to enter fully into God's project and become repairers of the world.

As we encounter Christ in word and sacrament, in our fellowship with one another and our communion with God, let us ask ourselves this: How is God inviting us—inviting me—into God's jubilee *shalom?* What in me—in the church—needs to be repaired and transformed in order for me—for us—to enter wholeheartedly into God's work of repairing the world?

O God of unchangeable power and eternal light: Look favorably on your whole Church, that wonderful and sacred mystery; by the effectual working of your providence, carry out in tranquillity the plan of salvation; let the whole world see and know that things which were cast down are being raised up, and things which had grown old are being made new, and that all things are being brought to their perfection by him through whom all things were made, your Son Jesus Christ our Lord; who lives and reigns with you, in the unity of the Holy Spirit, one God, for ever and ever. Amen.

Collect for Good Friday,
BCP 280

two

Going Home

In those days Jesus came from Nazareth of Galilee and was baptized by John in the Jordan. And just as he was coming up out of the water, he saw the heavens torn apart and the Spirit descending like a dove on him. And a voice came from heaven, "You are my Son, the Beloved; with you I am well pleased."

Mark 1:9-11

Y ou shall hallow the fiftieth year and you shall proclaim liberty throughout the land to all its inhabitants. It shall be a jubilee for you: you shall return, every one of you, to your property and every one of you to your family" (Leviticus 25:10). In short, you shall go home. Go home: back to your roots, back to the source. "That fiftieth year shall be a jubilee for you: you shall not sow, or reap the aftergrowth, or harvest the unpruned vines. For it is a jubilee; it shall be holy to you: you shall eat only what the field itself produces" (Leviticus 25:11-12).

In these words, "the sabbath rest"—that time of recreation and restoration—is extended. And not only are all set at liberty, but they are to return home, to where it all began. They are to go back and recover their sense of identity in their ancestral soil: the olive grove, the pasture, the familiar yet forgotten forest—home. In its own way, the land, too, is allowed to go home, to return to its natural state, to recover its equilibrium and undergo repair. It is released from usefulness and the self-serving manipulations of those who sow and reap. Nothing during the jubilee year can be harvested and one can only eat what the soil produces of its own accord.

When we set aside times in our lives for rest or retreat, for quiet reflection or laughter and play, we are setting ourselves free from sowing and reaping the fruits of our work. This may make some of us uneasy, because this is, after all, how we often find our meaning and purpose: we make decisions, we work to support our families and our common life. But we must step back at times and consider the fundamental decisions that ground all else that we do. These decisions are about what it really means to be the people of God, what it means to be called, to incarnate the compassion of Christ and to live lives of communion. How can we live in that communion, revealing the unyielding and tenacious love that passes ceaselessly from the Father to the Son and from the Son to the Father in the Holy Spirit?

This communion is not our creation. It is the inner dynamic of God's own life. God's own life and being are shared with us in baptism, and deepened and nurtured in the eucharist, the communion of the body and blood of Christ, in

13

which we are bound not only to Christ but to one another.

Communion is God's deepest desire for us; communion is to go home, to return to our roots, to reclaim who we are and are called to be in grace and truth. And therefore we need to have regular opportunities to release ourselves from useful productivity and purposeful accomplishment and to let Christ, through the agency of the Spirit, lead us home, back to our roots as persons of faith, back to those places and moments in our lives when the Hound of Heaven nipped us in the heel and God laid claim to us and called us by name.

In order to make this journey home, let us look to Jesus, "the pioneer and perfecter of our faith," as we are told in the letter to the Hebrews, and learn from him who is the way, the truth, and the life. Where do we start? We begin with Jesus in maturity undergoing baptism at the hands of John. This is where the gospel of Mark, the earliest of the four gospels, begins: with Jesus' baptism and the descent of the Spirit and a voice from heaven saying, "You are my Son, the Beloved; with you I am well pleased" (1:11). Notice that at

that shattering moment no task is assigned, no
agenda given, no test prescribed. Jesus is simply
loved by God wildly and with divine abandon.
Nothing—and I stress *nothing*—is asked for or
required of Jesus other than to accept God's
delight and pleasure in his very being.

Does God delight in you? Have you ever dared
to ask the question? Do you *let* God delight in
you?

It is worth noting that the Greek word in
scripture for "to will" also means to take pleasure
in and feel affection for. We have so reduced and
so limited notions of God's will to orders and
commands—"do this, do that"—that we have
lost sight of the truth that God's will is funda-
mentally a matter of divine affection and delight.

Those of you who are parents might think of
yourselves in relationship to your children. As
your children grow to maturity, what is your will
for them? It is not that they perfectly obey your
every thought and command. Your will for them
is your desire for their flourishing, their happi-
ness. And you agonize with them when they seem
to be going in a wrong direction and you rejoice
with them when things go well. That is your will

for your children: their deepest well-being. And that is God's fundamental will for us. In the same way, Jesus' identity and self-understanding, born at that baptismal moment, is rooted and grounded in knowing that he is loved infinitely by God, whom he addressed in answering love as Abba, father.

16

I think our greatest sin against the Holy Spirit is to deny God's love which, Paul tells us, is poured into our hearts by the Holy Spirit. And here I would point out that Karl Menninger, that great figure in American mental health, once observed that from his perspective the primary cause of mental illness lies in people's "inability to forgive themselves for being imperfect." Think about it.

Scripture helps us here, too, to see how we resist and push against that deep love that God seeks to enfold us in. A verse in the letter to the Hebrews is normally translated in this fashion: "Consider him who endured such hostility against himself from sinners" (12:3). But if you read the variant text printed at the bottom of the page, which may well be older than the official text, you hear these words: "Consider him who endured such hostility from sinners against them-selves." Self-directed hostility, I think, is one of the great sins of the church.

In the Revelation to John, Satan is presented as the one who accuses our comrades night and day before God. And I think here of the interior voice of accusation that resides within so many of us, always finding fault instead of driving us into the arms of God's mercy. This accusing voice turns us more and more into ourselves in a spirit of hostil-ity and self-accusation, which then gets projected outward onto others. I think much of the anger in society and in the church comes from this pro-jected self-castigation.

Here I would point out that as you look at the gospel you can see that genuine remorse, genuine repentance, opens us to God, whereas self-hatred imprisons us more and more within ourselves. Look at Peter and Judas: Peter, who repents and is able then to enter into the abiding love of the risen Christ, and Judas, who simply turns within himself and destroys himself. Our liberation and our homecoming is to let God say to each one of us, "You are my beloved; with you I am well pleased." Our identity, our true identity, is that we are deeply, profligately, and irresponsibly loved by God. Jubilee is a time to go home to that love.

Some years ago I went on retreat with a group of young clergy to a Benedictine monastery outside Elmira, New York. We were all full of ourselves. We had the answers to all the church's and the world's problems. Most of us were curates having to endure the idiocies of rectors who were out of date. At the end of the retreat the ancient abbot picked up his Bible and read to us from the book of Revelation the words of the risen Christ to the angel of the church in Ephesus. And this is what Christ says:

> I know your works, your toil and your patient endurance. I know that you cannot tolerate evildoers; you have tested those who claim to be apostles but are not, and have found them to be false. I also know that you are enduring patiently and bearing up for the sake of my name, and that you have not grown weary. (Revelation 2:2-3)

We all saw ourselves in that wonderful picture of absolute faithfulness and hard work. And then a curious smile played across the abbot's face and he went on: "But I have this against you, that you have abandoned the love you had at first." And every one of us was convicted. All of us, in one way or another, had become technicians of the sacred, manipulators of the things of God, and had lost that awareness of having been called, of being deeply loved by God.

It is very easy for all of us in the church, lay and ordained, to become technicians of the sacred, to lose contact with the root and ground of our faith: the very love that animates and gives authenticity and validity to our words and our actions and gives power to the gospel we seek to proclaim.

There at the waters of the Jordan, Jesus knew who he was, with no agenda given—he simply knew that he was deeply loved. And here we are: the people of God, baptized into Christ, limbs of Christ's risen body, each of us with our own identity, vocation, and mission—an identity that is rooted and grounded in God's boundless love for each one of us, a love we seldom dare to claim.

I think here of a poem written in the seventeeth century by an Anglican priest, George

Herbert, a country parson who lived near the city of Salisbury in England. He intimately knew something about struggling with the tenaciousness of God's love. He writes:

> Love bade me welcome: yet my soul
> > drew back,
> Guilty of dust and sin.

Where was the poet's focus? His focus was on himself.

> But quick-ey'd Love, observing me
> > grow slack
> From my first entrance in,
> Drew nearer to me, sweetly questioning,
> If I lack'd anything.
> A guest, I answer'd, worthy to be here:
> Love said, You shall be he.
> I the unkind, ungrateful? Ah my dear,
> I cannot look on thee.
> Love took my hand, and smiling did reply,
> Who made the eyes but I?
> Truth Lord, but I have marr'd them: let
> > my shame
> Go where it doth deserve.

20

See how he clings to guilt and shame.

> And know you not, says Love, who bore
> the blame?

And then the poet does what we so often try to do: "All right, God; I will let you love me if I can do something that will allow me to feel that I am worthy of being loved. If I can accomplish something worthy in my own sight, then I can accept, in some way, that you love me." And that is what the poet means when he says,

> My dear, then I will serve.

But Love, as the risen Christ, has had enough of this and says,

> You must sit down, says Love, and taste
> my meat:
> So I did sit and eat.

Struggle and yielding to the divine Love. So I invite you to see jubilee, as I said before, as an invitation to go home: an invitation to return to God's love—to accept your own belovedness, with warts, imperfections, and all. Remember what Christ says to St. Paul, who was embarrassed by a thorn in his flesh. It was a burden that he was reluctant to carry, and so Paul says, "Take it away and then I can really feel that I am free— that I truly am in the new creation." And Christ says: "No. It stays. My grace is all you need; my power comes before realization, not when you think you are strong and perfect, but in the midst of your weakness."

Allow God to love you. I think that is the invitation of today. Maybe there have been moments in your life when you have known that love, but you have completely forgotten how it feels. Perhaps fear or busyness or professional responsibilities have occluded that awareness. Maybe that belovedness has been mediated to you through people around you whom you take for granted but you need to give thanks for. You need to go back to your roots, go back home again and remember that belovedness. "You are my beloved; with you I am well pleased.

○

O love, how deep, how broad, how high,
 how passing thought and fantasy,
that God, the Son of God, should take
 our mortal form for mortals' sake.

For us baptized, for us he bore
 his holy fast and hungered sore;
for us temptations sharp he knew;
 for us the tempter overthrew.

For us he prayed; for us he taught;
 for us his daily works he wrought:
by words and signs and actions, thus
 still seeking not himself, but us.

For us to wicked hands betrayed,
 scourged, mocked, in purple robe
  arrayed,
he bore the shameful cross and death;
 for us gave up his dying breath.

For us he rose from death again;
    for us he went on high to reign;
for us he sent his Spirit here
    to guide, to strengthen, and to cheer.

All glory to our Lord and God
    for love so deep, so high, so broad;
the Trinity whom we adore
    for ever and for evermore.

Latin, fifteenth century;
Hymn 448 in The Hymnal 1982

◊

three

In the Wilderness

And the Spirit immediately drove Jesus out into the wilderness. He was in the wilderness forty days, tempted by Satan; and he was with the wild beasts; and the angels waited on him.

Mark 1:12-13

Following Jesus' baptism, with the voice from heaven still ringing in his ears, that same Spirit who bore down upon him in the waters of baptism drives him out into the wilderness. This is one continuous action on the part of the Spirit. And there in the wilderness, as we well know, Jesus faces temptation: the fundamental temptation to possess and claim as his own his newly experienced sense of belovedness, claiming it as something to cling to and to enjoy on his own terms. In the wilderness Jesus struggles with the question, "How do I respond in answering love to this overwhelming sense of belovedness? How do I receive it as gift, not as possession?" I think here of the words of Paul in the letter to the Philippians:

> Let the same mind be in you that was in Christ Jesus, who, though he was in the form of God, did not regard equality with God as something to be exploited, but emptied himself. (Philippians 2:5-7)

He did not cling to his belovedness, but offered it freely in the service of Abba.

There in the wilderness the Spirit, with the assistance of Satan, helps Jesus explore and recognize his own potential patterns of self-assertion and ego gratification that could undermine the relationship of belovedness. The wilderness then becomes an occasion of self-knowledge and wisdom so that Jesus can move from the wilderness into his ministry, where he will be tempted again and again yet can return to the deep knowing that came to him in the wilderness. "One does not live by bread alone," Jesus says to the devil, "but by every word that comes from the mouth of God" (Matthew 4:4).

Jesus emerges from the wilderness not only with a sense of his identity but now with a sense of vocation. This vocation is, I think, best expressed in John's gospel where Jesus says, "My food is to do the will of him who sent me and to complete"—to accomplish and fulfill—"his work" (4:34). "Something's your vocation," writes novelist Gail Godwin in *Evensong,* "if it keeps making more of you."[2] So Jesus' vocation is not simply a path; it is the way in which he will grow more deeply into his own identity. And so, too, with us, if something is genuinely a vocation, it may be burdensome at times but its demands will not ultimately diminish us; they will increase us and lead us more fully into the selfhood that God desires for us.

Jesus' radical availability to God's will, Abba's loving desire, was the way in which he discovered who he was and became more and more himself. Then Jesus, filled with the power of the Spirit, returned to Galilee with a sense of his identity and a sense of his vocation. And we find him, in Luke's gospel, returning to the hometown synagogue. My sense is that as he entered the room there was a sort of whispering around the edges: "He's back...He looks a little gaunt," some of the mothers might have said—after all, he had been fasting in the wilderness forty days and forty nights. And then the president of the synagogue, relieved that one of the hometown boys who had disappeared for a while is finally home again, hands him the scroll and invites him to do the free reading for the day.

We do not know whether Jesus already had in mind the opening verses of the sixty-first chapter of the prophet Isaiah, or whether he simply unrolled the scroll and there they were. In any event, he picked up the scroll and read: "The Spirit of the Lord is upon me, because he has anointed me"—and he could say, "in my baptism"—"to bring good news to the poor. He has sent me to proclaim release to the captives and recovery of sight to the blind, to let the oppressed go free, to proclaim the year of the Lord's favor" (Luke 4:18-19). I am sure he read the words with a kind of authority and urgency that made the reading much more than just another reading. My sense is that as he read those words, he knew the content and direction of his mission. Identity, vocation, and mission now all came together as the word of God leapt off the page, embraced him, and said, "This is your life: this is the meaning of what you have been called to do."

29

He rolled up the scroll, gave it back to the attendant, and sat down. The eyes of all in the synagogue were fixed on him, and he must have been aware of that. A silence pervaded the synagogue. Something had happened—though no one knew exactly what. As Jesus takes the word of scripture into himself, he allows it to find a home at the heart of his own identity and his sense of vocation: *my food is to do the will of the one who sent me and to complete his work.* He says simply, "Today this scripture has been fulfilled in your hearing" (Luke 4:21).

And with that, jubilee becomes the absolute center of his ministry and every single thing that happens beyond that point, including his free leaping onto the cross, is in the service of jubilee—in the service of release, freedom, reconciliation, re-creation. And so there is *no way whatsoever* we as Christians can avoid jubilee. Jesus is the personification of the Lord's favor. "For freedom Christ has set us free," says Paul in the letter to the Galatians (5:1). Do we dare enter into and claim that freedom?

What is your vocation: what is your deepest desire as a person of faith? Is your food to do the will of God—that is, to enter into God's gracious and affectionate yearning for your flourishing in accordance with God's own project? Is your sense of vocation rooted in a sense that "my food is to do the will of the One who sent me and to complete his work"? And then your mission, the way that you live out that vocation: how are you called to proclaim the good news of jubilee in remission and forgiveness? By undoing indebted-

30

ness, setting others free from those judgments that we cling to and define them by. There is so much suspicion and hostility in the church, and alas, there are those who delight in misrepresentation and in spreading ill report. And there are still others of us who delight in reading about it, especially when it is about people we do not like.

So, where do we need to turn jubilee from some cosmic abstraction into a practical discipline of forgiveness that we extend to one another? There may be someone who terrifies us, whom we have judged as beyond what we have perceived to be the boundaries of the Christian community. Do we need to seek that person out, or some person who represents that community? Do we need to say, "I'm sorry. I welcome you in the freedom of Christ. I welcome you in the belovedness with which God welcomes me"?

What do you need to set yourself free from? What is God inviting you to allow to pass away? What judgments and assumptions and suspicions is God asking you to give up? All of this, however, flows from our own belovedness. We cannot extend to others what we have not, in some sense, received ourselves. And the love of God can heal us and transform us as no other power, no other force in this world, possibly can.

32

Almighty and everlasting God, whose will it is to restore all things in your well-beloved Son, the King of kings and Lord of lords: Mercifully grant that the peoples of the earth, divided and enslaved by sin, may be freed and brought together under his most gracious rule; who lives and reigns with you and the Holy Spirit, one God, now and for ever.

Collect for Proper 29,
BCP 236

◊

four

Grace Upon Grace

*There is therefore now no condemnation
for those who are in Christ Jesus. For the
law of the Spirit of life in Christ Jesus has
set you free from the law of sin and of
death.... Who will bring any charge
against God's elect? It is God who justifies.
Who is to condemn? It is Christ Jesus, who
died, yes, who was raised, who is at the right
hand of God, who indeed intercedes for us.*

Romans 8:1-2, 33-34

In his letter to the Christians in Rome, Paul tells us that in Christ we are freed from condemnation: our own and that of others. In much the same vein, a number of centuries later Julian of Norwich—that remarkable and altogether free (in a gospel sense) woman of prayer and deep insight—wrote that she believed "there is no wrath in God . . . for I saw no whit of anger in God—in short or in long term." She continued, "In God's sight we do not fall, in our sight we do not stand. As I see it both of these are true, but the deeper insight belongs to God."

Julian's experience of God in Christ ran quite counter to the dominant religious sensibilities of the fifteenth century in which she lived, and that experience worked in her a boldness and a daring—an interior confidence nurtured by prayer and the sacramental life of the church—that allowed her to say with humble assurance, "As I see it." As I see it there is no condemnation, there is no wrath; instead, there is all compassion. This compassion was made flesh and dwells among us in Jesus Christ through the Holy Spirit.

This is not good news: it is shocking news. It is threatening news to those who make their living by warding off the divine wrath through rites and ceremonies and systems of sacrifice. No wonder Jesus was done in.

"Humankind cannot stand very much reality," observed the poet T. S. Eliot. And what humankind can bear least of all is the unbounded, unselective, and sovereign freedom of the divine compassion.

I think here of the parable of the workers in the vineyard: the ones employed at the end of the day received the same wage as those hired at dawn. "Unfair," the latter group complain. "Are you envious because I am generous?" the landowner replies.

God's generosity is revealed in God's compassion: it is the "fullness" we receive, the "grace upon grace" that is ours in Christ. There is no condemnation for those who are in Christ Jesus. Dare we live this as true? Dare we live it personally and as a church? Is not this our vocation?

And what is compassion, but to suffer with and enter into another's truth, another's joys and burdens, another's ambiguities and paradoxes, another's struggles to be faithful, another's moments of grace and imperfection? To welcome others in the power of the love with which Christ loves us and gave himself for us is to give others room in which to reveal and not simply defend themselves.

"I will listen to what the LORD God is saying," the psalmist tells us, "for he is speaking peace to his faithful people and to those who turn their hearts to him" (85:8). Where are our hearts? Are they turned? Remember: conversation and conversion open the way to our being turned. Are we ready to hear what God is saying, perhaps through the all-too-human voice of another? "Out beyond ideas of wrongdoing and rightdoing, there is a field. I'll meet you there," declares the Sufi mystic and poet Rumi.[3] Are we ready to make the journey to that field? Are we ready to enter that open place the psalms speak of, where compassion embraces us in communion, where "mercy and truth have met together; righteousness and peace have kissed each other" (85:10)? Are we ready to discover that all of us—bound and free, Jew and Greek, male and female—are one, in ways that pass all understanding? One, not in some feat of human joinery, but one in the power and force of God's desire. Compassion is not simply a divine attribute, it reveals the very nature of God.

In Luke's gospel we hear the story of the healing of a woman who has been bent over for eighteen years (13:10-17). "You are set free," Jesus declares to her as he lays his hands upon her. And the woman who has suffered for so long stands up straight and praises God. It is the sabbath, though, and the leader of the synagogue, who sees only the law, is scandalized: "There are six days on which work ought to be done; come on those days and be cured, and not on the sabbath day." But Jesus' work, which is Abba's work, is sabbath work: "Ought not this woman, a daughter of Abraham whom Satan bound for eighteen long years, be set free from this bondage on the sabbath day?"

Jesus makes no apologies. He is engaged in sabbathing, jubilee work, setting free, raising up, making whole, making new. Compassion is his very food. And it is ours as well, so we might ask ourselves: what must be released in us in order to stand straight and to welcome God's compassion? Why is God's compassion at times a threat? What bent-over attitudes and perceptions and practices must be acknowledged in me and in us in order to surrender, to die, to let go, and thereby enter into the new space, the open field where there is no condemnation "because there is no whit of anger in God—in short or in long term"?

There's a wideness in God's mercy
    like the wideness of the sea;
there's a kindness in his justice,
    which is more than liberty.
There is welcome for the sinner,
    and more graces for the good;
there is mercy with the Savior;
    there is healing in his blood.

There is no place where earth's sorrows
    are more felt than up in heaven;
there is no place where earth's failings
    have such kindly judgment given.
There is plentiful redemption
    in the blood that has been shed;

there is joy for all the members
    in the sorrows of the Head.

For the love of God is broader
    than the measure of the mind;
and the heart of the Eternal
    is most wonderfully kind.
If our love were but more faithful,
    we should take him at his word;
and our life would be thanksgiving
    for the goodness of the Lord.

Frederick William Faber,
Hymn 470 in The Hymnal 1982

◊

five

Be Not Afraid

The angel Gabriel came to Mary and said, "Greetings, favored one! The Lord is with you." But she was much perplexed by his words and pondered what sort of greeting this might be. The angel said to her, "Do not be afraid, Mary, for you have found favor with God. . . . Then Mary said, "Here am I, the servant of the Lord; let it be with me according to your word."

Luke 1:28-30, 38

D
o not fear, do not be afraid," the angel Gabriel says to Mary. "There is no fear in love, but perfect love casts out fear," the author of the first letter of John tells us. "We love because God first loved us" (1 John 4:18-19). The Cistercian writer Guillaume de Saint Thierry wrote many centuries ago:

> You loved us first so that we might love you. And this was not because you needed to be loved by us, but because we could not be what you created us to be unless we loved you.

Loving the God who first loves us is not a duty, one of the many oughts and shoulds and musts with which we afflict ourselves. Instead, loving God is integral to our full humanity. It is part of the fundamental structure of our personhood.

Love shatters our defenses and opens us to surprise and possibility beyond our wildest imagining. Love gives us courage and confidence and boldness. Boldness is one of the fruits of the resurrection that overtakes the apostles in the book of Acts, laying claim to them and drawing them beyond themselves, giving them the gift of plain and direct and confident speech. They are given the capacity to bear witness to the Risen One in the face of threat and opposition without fear and without losing heart.

I think here of the words of Paul in the letter to the Romans:

> Suffering produces endurance, and endurance produces character, and character produces hope, and hope does not disappoint us, because God's love has been poured into our hearts through the Holy Spirit that has been given to us. (Romans 5:3-5)

Character is the result of endurance, of having passed through the fire, of having remained steadfast even in the very midst of hell without despair. It is God's love, poured into our hearts by the Spirit, that gives us the capacity to endure in the face of drastic and demanding circumstances. In some elemental way that passes all understanding we know with Julian of Norwich that "all shall be well, and all shall be well, and all manner of things shall be well." Such is the hidden power of love that draws us on, draws us deeper into God's own life and overcomes all fear.

"Do not be afraid," the angel Gabriel says to Mary as he announces that she shall bear a son, God's chosen one. And yet in the midst of her being deeply troubled and perplexed, Mary is able to stammer, "Let it be with me according to your word." And with that her journey begins. She not only bears the Word and follows the Word and finds that her soul is pierced by the Word as he hangs upon the cross, but she is refashioned by the Word in the wind and fire of Pentecost as she waits with the apostles in the upper room. She is deeply perplexed not once but over and over again by the one she calls her son, always mindful of old Simeon's prophecy about being pierced by a sword because of her child.

She had much to ponder in her heart: his disappearance into the wilderness, the hostility of the town, her doubts about his sanity when people said, as we are told in Mark, "He has gone out of his mind." No, it did not end with his birth or his growing up: it only got stranger and wilder. And yet she suffered for him and with him and because of him, and she endured—growing there-

43

by into the mystery of her own character: her own identity, vocation, and mission.

Bearing the Word into life and through death into resurrection, her son rising within her own self, Mary knew the power of Jesus' resurrection by sharing his sufferings, to echo words of Paul. Beyond her fear and perplexity—or better yet, at the heart of her fear and perplexity—the love within her, provoked by God's loving favor and delight announced by an angel—"Greetings, favored one, the Lord is with you"—moved Mary to say, *"Fiat;* so be it, yes." And yet, once said, that "yes" had to be repeated at every turning of the way, right up to the foot of the cross.

Remembering and pondering the angel's greeting in her heart, "the Lord is with you," was the ground of her hope, her deep confidence that "all shall be well, and all shall be well, and all manner of things shall be well"—beyond her comprehension but according to God's own desire. It was this deep knowing that led Mary on in answering availability to all that life set before her.

To enter into the open space, the field of jubilee obliges us to pass through the narrow door of our fears: the fear that if I listen deeply I may lose my own certitude; the fear that if I make room for the other, I may lose my singularity and uniqueness; the fear that if I truly open my heart I will lose control and be taken beyond myself; the fear that if I live the mystery—God's mystery—of release, remission, and reconciliation I will have nothing left to call my own.

45

Though deeply troubled and perplexed, our sister Mary risked all by saying "yes." What about you? "Greetings, favored one! The Lord is with you," God says to each one of us. What fears must we face and relinquish in order to say "yes" to God's project of reordering, restoring, and making all things one?

O God, you made us in your own image and redeemed us through Jesus your Son: Look with compassion on the whole human family; take away the arrogance and hatred which infect our hearts; break down the

walls that separate us; unite us in bonds of love; and work through our struggle and confusion to accomplish your purposes on earth; that, in your good time, all nations and races may serve you in harmony around your heavenly throne; through Jesus Christ our Lord. Amen.

Prayer for the Human Family,
BCP 815

six

A Compassionate Heart

The LORD is full of compassion
and mercy,
slow to anger and of great kindness.
He will not always accuse us,
nor will he keep his anger for ever.
He has not dealt with us according to
our sins
nor rewarded us according to our
wickedness.

For as the heavens are high above
>the earth,
>>so is his mercy great upon those
>>who fear him.
As far as the east is from the west,
>so far has he removed our sins
>>from us.

Psalm 103:8-12

Forgiveness lies at the very heart of jubilee because "the LORD is full of compassion and mercy"; indeed, "as far as the east is from the west, so far has he removed our sins from us." Compassion is God's very name; compassion is God's very nature. Compassion is Jesus' words and deeds. Compassion is Jesus on the cross—his arms of love stretched out so that everyone might come within the reach of his saving embrace.

"Be perfect, therefore, as your heavenly Father is perfect," Jesus instructs the crowds in the Sermon on the Mount (Matthew 5:48). In what is largely the same discourse delivered in the gospel of Luke, not on a mountain top but on a level place, Jesus instructs the crowds to "be merciful, just as your Father is merciful" (Luke 6:36). Could it be that the two commands, so similar in construction and context, are in fact one and the same? Is being perfect—or, more properly, being complete, mature, fully grown-up into Christ who is our life—is that being merciful and compassionate in the power of God's own mercy and compassion?

According to the desert tradition of the fourth century, the principal discipline of the serious Christian is the acquisition of a heart: "Acquire a heart and you shall be saved," we are told. In scripture and the ascetical tradition of the church the heart is understood as the core and center of our personhood. If the heart, therefore, is filled with evil treasure, Jesus tells us, a person produces evil, and if the heart is filled with good treasure, the result is good, "for it is out of the abundance of the heart that the mouth speaks" (Luke 6:45).

The acquisition of a heart is a lifelong process of ongoing conversion. In this process we are turned by others, by the events of our lives, by

God's grace in all its maddening and unpredictable manifestations—turned away from our carefully tended and defended self-constructions toward the inexhaustible mystery of God whose ways are not our ways. We are turned "till by turning, turning we come round right," as the Shaker hymn expresses it.

"Consider the work of God," declares the writer of Ecclesiastes, "who can make straight what he has made crooked?" (Ecclesiastes 7:13). And yet how often we try to force God's ways to fit our logic, our patterns of consistency, and thereby attempt to construct a church that is not the body of Christ but the projection of our own egos, whatever our points of view may be.

One of the painful joys of being limbs of one body, living stones of one building is that we need each other to be the whole body growing to maturity in Christ—a spiritual temple, a spiritual house, of God's continuing construction. Acquiring a merciful and compassionate heart renders us permeable not only to God's imagination and God's perspective, but to what Paul calls God's foolishness: a foolishness made manifest in

Christ crucified, a foolishness that is wiser than human wisdom.

This foolish compassion extends to every aspect of our lives. In Deuteronomy, for example, we hear that keeping jubilee involves the remission of debt, our forgiveness rendered concrete as an expression of the unboundaried forgiveness of God:

> Every seventh year you shall grant a remission of debts. And this is the manner of the remission: every creditor shall remit the claim that is held against a neighbor, not exacting it of a neighbor who is a member of the community, because the LORD's remission has been proclaimed. (Deuteronomy 15:1-2)

Indeed, this passage speaks not only of remission of debt, of being set free from financial bondage, but of release from the bonds of slavery. Slaves were to be set free in the seventh year, and that freedom rendered concrete the freedom of the Lord's redemption. Further, freedom was to be accompanied by acts of liberality: the former slaves were not to be sent out empty-handed.

Provide liberally out of your flock, your threshing floor, and your wine press, thus giving to him some of the bounty with which the LORD your God has blessed you. Remember that you were a slave in the land of Egypt, and the LORD your God redeemed you; for this reason I lay this command upon you today. (Deuteronomy 15:14-15)

In our culture of ruthless and unrestrained acquisition, we never seem to have enough. There is always more we want: something newer, bigger, more in style. Yet the more we have, the more bound and anxious we become. The gift of a merciful and compassionate heart can, however, set us free, as God's compassion, working in us by the Spirit, undoes and refashions the spirit of our minds (Ephesians 4:23).

How do we acquire a compassionate heart? We pray for one, and open ourselves to repentance—repentance that means "to adopt God's point of view in place of your own," as William Temple neatly puts it. He then goes on to say, "There need not be any sorrow about [repentance]. In itself, far from being sorrowful, it is the most joyful thing in the world, because when you have done it you have adopted the viewpoint of truth itself, and you are in fellowship with God." To adopt the viewpoint of truth itself, the truth as in Jesus who is the truth, is to be rendered merciful, to be made complete.

Many centuries ago St. Issac of Syria was asked, "What is a merciful heart?" This was his reply:

It is a heart that burns with love for the whole of creation—for men and women, for the birds, for the beasts, for the demons, for every creature. When a person with a heart such as this thinks of the creatures or looks at them, his eyes are filled with tears. An overwhelming compassion makes his heart grow small and weak, and he cannot endure to hear or see any suffering, even the smallest pain, inflicted upon any creature. Therefore he never ceases to pray, with tears even for the irrational animals, for the enemies of truth, and for those who do him evil, asking that they may be guarded and receive God's mercy. And for the reptiles also he prays with a

great compassion which rises up endlessly
in his heart until he shines again and is glorious like God.

A merciful heart can embrace everything,
everything, everything. Paradox, contradiction,
fear, hatred, even evil itself, as Christ did on the
cross when he cried out, "Father, forgive them;
for they do not know what they are doing." A
merciful heart, because it is one with the heart of
Christ, can bear all things, believe all things, hope
all things, endure all things, to echo Paul. It is a
heart that eagerly grants remission and provides
liberally not out of its own meager store but out
of God's rich and generous mercy.

"Give me a heart of inexhaustible tenderness,"
prayed Francis of Assisi. Am I able to make his
prayer my own? Not in the future, when all is
peaceful and calm, but right now, in the midst of
my life, with all its hopes and fears, its moments
of sinfulness and malevolence, as well as its glim-
mers of goodness and grace?

◊

Lord, make us instruments of your peace. Where there is hatred, let us sow love; where there is injury, pardon; where there is discord, union; where there is doubt, faith; where there is despair, hope; where there is darkness, light; where there is sadness, joy. Grant that we may not so much seek to be consoled as to console; to be understood as to understand; to be loved as to love. For it is in giving that we receive; it is in pardoning that we are pardoned; and it is in dying that we are born to eternal life. Amen.

A prayer attributed to St. Francis,
BCP 833

seven

A School for the Lord's Service

My child, if you accept my words
    and treasure up my commandments
      within you,
making your ear attentive to wisdom
    and inclining your heart to
      understanding;
if you indeed cry out for insight,
    and raise your voice for
      understanding; . . .

then you will understand righteousness
 and justice and equity,
  every good path;
for wisdom will come into your heart,
 and knowledge will be pleasant to
  your soul;
prudence will watch over you;
 and understanding will guard you.

Proverbs 2:1-3, 9-11

*O*bsculta, listen: so begins the Rule of St. Benedict, who is considered the father of western monasticism. "Listen...with the ear of the heart," he instructs his followers. "Let us open our eyes to the light that comes from God, and our ears to the voice from heaven that every day calls out this charge: If you hear his voice today, do not harden your hearts." Benedict's rule, written in the sixth century, and drawing largely from an earlier rule, the Rule of the Master, sets forth the journey into Christ in terms of listening. The context for listening is a commu-

nity gathered together under the care and over-
sight of an *abba,* a father, an abbot who represents Christ.

The community itself is described as "a school
for the Lord's service." It is not a place, but rather
a closely knit group, as in a school of fish who are
devoted to a common vocation: moving together
in the same direction. In this case, the common
vocation is living out in community and through
the very experience of community, in all its
demanding concreteness, the baptismal mystery
of dying and rising with Christ.

One of the distinctive vows of a Benedictine
monk or nun is that of stability, staying put and
accepting the fact that one's brother and one's sister, in all their singularity and sometimes contrary
opinions, are the chosen instruments of one's conversion of life, one's being turned toward Christ.
Our faults and foibles, as well as our capacity for
grace and truth, are brought to light through the
unavoidable intimacies of communal life. Though
this is true in a particularly intense way in a
monastic community, it is also true of the various
configurations of communal ecclesial life with
which we are familiar—from the local congrega-

tion to the diocese and national church to the world-wide Anglican Communion.

What does Benedict's rule have to teach us about keeping jubilee? What wisdom and insight does Benedict—who describes himself as "a father who loves you"—have to impart to us? Listen carefully to everything, he tells us.

Listen to the patient wisdom of the elders, the urgency of the young, the constructive insight of the visitor who may see the community from the outside with a clarity denied to those who are caught up in its daily preoccupations.

Listen to the abbot, who, following the example of Christ, is called to be the servant of all: challenging the strong and making allowance for the weak.

Listen to Christ in the daily patterns of work and prayer marking the hours of the day: to Christ who rises like the dawn and meets us in word and sacrament; to Christ who encounters us in our brothers and sisters and the seemingly ordinary events of the day. Everything, according to Benedict, conspires to open the ear of our hearts in order to hear God's voice.

But there is another aspect of the Rule that is equally important: its sense of moderation and balance. Benedict, according to his biographer Gregory the Great, had begun his life of following Christ as a cave-dwelling hermit in the wilderness of Subicao, some forty miles west of Rome. Filled with the zeal of the fourth-century desert monastics, he was tireless in his discipline and self-denial.

When asked by a group of wayward monks at a nearby monastery to become their abbot, he warned them that his "way of life would never harmonize with theirs." They persisted in their invitation, however. He accepted and instituted such stringent reforms that they attempted to poison his wine. "May Almighty God have mercy upon you. Go find yourself an abbot to your own liking," he said, returning to his "beloved wilderness." He returned somewhat wiser, I believe, and more ready to accept the fact that if you strain the bow string too far, as his monastic forebear, Antony of Egypt, had once observed, the bow will snap. So, too, with any of us, if we are pressed beyond the limits of our own humanity.

When you compare the Rule of Benedict with its precursor, the Rule of the Master, Benedict's desire "to set down nothing harsh, nothing burdensome" reveals itself in any number of allowances he makes for diverse personalities and aptitudes and degrees of maturity.

Benedict's Rule seeks to establish the rhythms of a disciplined life that is ordered to the slow but exacting developmental process of growing up into Christ. Benedict wanted to avoid the distortions of an exaggerated zeal or an overweening perfectionism, which can devolve easily into ruthless judgment of self and others. The Rule represents, I think, Benedict's own struggle with Satan masquerading as an angel of light—that is, evil tempting us under the guise of some greater good, some more perfect way that altogether rejects the thorns in the flesh, the weaknesses, the idiocies that God lovingly accepts as part of who we are.

"Never despair of God's mercy," Benedict declared. I would not be surprised if he wrote those words as much for himself as for his monks. If zeal, no matter how noble it may sound, strays from the path of mercy and ignores our human frailty, it is not of God.

In Luke's gospel, Jesus tells us that "none of you can become my disciple if you do not give up all your possessions" (14:33). Perhaps the possessions we most need to give up are the idols of our own righteousness and the idealized self I yearn to be that refuses to acknowledge the imperfect self God calls "beloved." The "sound wisdom" of Benedict is a much needed corrective. Obsculta— let us listen attentively with the ear of the heart and make it our own, for we too, the church, the body of Christ, are a school for the Lord's service.

Day by day, dear Lord,
    of thee three things I pray:
to see thee more clearly,
    love thee more dearly,
follow thee more nearly,
    day by day.

Attributed to Richard of Chichester,
Hymn 654 in The Hymnal 1982

◊

eight

Now I See

Jesus said, "Therefore I tell you, do not worry about your life, what you will eat or what you will drink, or about your body, what you will wear. Is not life more than food, and the body more than clothing? Look at the birds of the air; they neither sow nor reap nor gather into barns, and yet your heavenly Father feeds them. Are you not of more value than they? And can any of you by worrying add a single hour to your span of life? And why do you worry about clothing? Consider the lilies of the field, how they grow; they neither toil nor spin, yet I tell you, even Solomon in all his glory was not clothed like one of these. But if God so clothes the grass of the field, which is alive today and tomorrow is thrown into the oven, will he not much more clothe you—you of little faith?

Matthew 6:25-30

64

Why is it that jubilee, so concretely described in scripture in terms of remission, release, and reordering of relationships, remained for the people of Israel and still remains for us largely a hope, a dream, a yearning? Can it be because of the hardness of our hearts, the littleness of our faith? As a cosmic abstraction or a diffuse hope, we welcome jubilee. But as its conditions impose themselves upon the actual structures of our lives, we recoil and equivocate and find all manner of reasons to make compromises and modifications.

In the Spiritual Exercises of St. Ignatius of Loyola there is a meditation called the Two Standards. In it the person making his or her way through the exercises, which have to do with deepening our companionship with Christ, is invited to consider the Standard of Christ and the Standard of Satan. Each standard has its own particular dynamic: the way of Christ has to do with freedom, and the way of Satan with inversion and self-imprisonment.

The way of the evil one, whom Ignatius appropriately styles "the enemy of our human nature," has a dynamic of riches, honor, and pride. Riches in this context stands for our tendency to possess, to cling, to hold on to things. Honor has to do with our self-definition, our self-understanding derived from what we possess. And pride is seen as the world we construct for ourselves based on what we possess and how we define ourselves.

If this seems abstract, an example may help. I have been entrusted with the ministry of Presiding Bishop. I can define myself and determine my self-worth in terms of my role. My role can become a possession instead of a service entrusted to me for the sake of others. I can then create a constricted

little world of fuschia in which adulation and def-
erence feed my ego, and criticism or challenge are
seen as threats against which I must defend
myself. In such a state, self-protection and anxiety
become my way of seeing things; wariness and
suspicion become my responses to the larger
world beyond the fortress of my pride.

The Standard of Christ, on the other hand, has
a dynamic of non-possession in which all is
acknowledged as gift. Instead of building defenses to protect myself, my borders are made permeable because nothing is ultimately mine. All is
God's. All is gift, not only to me but for the well-
being of others as well. "Consider the lilies of the
field, how they grow," Jesus tells the crowd.
"They neither toil nor spin, yet I tell you, even
Solomon in all his glory was not clothed like one
of these" (Matthew 6:28-29).

In Leviticus the sabbatical year from which the
jubilee year evolved is not only a year of rest, it is
also a season of availability, in which borders are
open, gates flung wide, barriers thrown down and
all, including wild animals, are free to eat what
the land yields of its own and God's accord. In
addition, this season of the sabbatical year is an

interior disposition in which all anxiety and self-protection, all clinging to what is mine, is over-ruled by God's own generosity as it works its way through grace into my awareness, into my consciousness and my actions.

"Unawareness is the root of all evil," the wisdom of the desert tells us. And indeed, the primary tactic of the enemy of our human nature is not to propose gross patterns of behavior but to keep us unmindful and unaware: "That's just the way things are"; "It's none of my concern"; "What do you mean I'm biased?" These attitudes keep us from seeing clearly and without distortion.

If it is true that we are for one another's salvation, then it is God's intent that we rub against one another, confront one another with the truth of our lives, and break one another open to deeper levels of awareness that take us beyond ourselves and impart clearness of sight. This undistorted vision allows us to see things and ourselves as they are, in the unwavering light of Christ who is our truth.

Jubilee is not just another perspective, super-added to our present and often self-protective points of view, but a radical shift in how and what we see. Jubilee sets in motion a series of unsettling critiques that oblige us to ask: What is going on here—in my life, in my perceptions, in my being in the world? Jubilee forces us to acknowledge I was blind but now I see.

What I am talking about here is the mystery of conversion, scales falling from our eyes, as they did in the case of Paul. A change of heart, a turning in a new direction occasioned by grace that can pounce upon us without warning.

The prophet Isaiah describes unawareness in terms of self-justifying ritual that gives the illusion of mindfulness because of appropriate words and liturgical forms.

> What to me is the multitude of your sacrifices? says the LORD; I have had enough of burnt offerings of rams and the fat of fed beasts; I do not delight in the blood of bulls, or of lambs, or of goats.... Your new moons and your appointed festivals my soul hates; they have become a burden to me, I am weary of bearing them. When you stretch out your hands, I will hide my eyes from you; even though you make many prayers, I will not listen; your hands are

> full of blood. Wash yourselves; make your-
> selves clean; remove the evil of your doings
> from before my eyes; cease to do evil, learn
> to do good; seek justice, rescue the
> oppressed, defend the orphan, plead for the
> widow. (Isaiah 1:11, 14-17)

How often do we recite the confession with no notion of our sin and pray the Lord's Prayer with no forgiveness, or even the desire for it, in our hearts? Conversion, coming to awareness, is a break in our patterns. Old ways of thinking and perceiving are challenged by the Spirit of truth who draws from what is Christ's and makes it known to us. "Wash yourselves, make yourselves clean" is Isaiah's way of calling us to awareness, and conversion to a change of heart and direction.

Jesus' call to conversion takes a very different form in his conversation with Zacchaeus the tax collector. With "quick-ey'd love" Jesus glances up in the tree and addresses Zacchaeus, who thinks he is at a safe distance to observe without having to become involved. "Zacchaeus," Jesus says, "hurry and come down; for I must stay at your house today" (Luke 19:5). Caught by surprise, riveted by Jesus' ruthlessly gentle gaze, Zacchaeus comes down. He has been found out and called out of hiding into the light. Suddenly this tax collector, loathed by the people because he is in league with the Romans who have reduced Israel to an occupied territory, is called out of his isolation, an isolation imposed from without by the people and from within by his shame.

"Listen!" cries the risen Christ in the book of Revelation. "I am standing at the door, knocking; if you hear my voice and open the door, I will come in to you and eat with you, and you with me" (Revelation 3:20). The year of the Lord's favor in the person of Jesus, in whom all jubilee yearnings and hopes are fulfilled, suddenly and shatteringly breaks into Zacchaeus' life. "Hurry and come down, open the door, the door of your heart. I will come in to you and eat with you and you with me." Hurry down, cries Jesus, and Zacchaeus "who once was lost is now found."

Zacchaeus leaps down in unbounded joy to welcome the one who has so deeply welcomed him. The storehouse of his heart is cracked open as he encounters in Jesus his own belovedness, a belovedness proclaimed in the simple words "I must stay at your house today." And from his heart, transformed by Jesus' compassion, flows generosity: "Look, half of my possessions, Lord, I will give to the poor; and if I have defrauded anyone of anything, I will pay back four times as much." To which Jesus replies, "Today salvation"—the year of the Lord's favor—"has come to this house" (Luke 19:8-9).

71

Delivered from unawareness, Zacchaeus sees for the first time: sees the poor, sees the distortions in his own life. He sees in the fierce light of the Divine Compassion that has embraced him that, in spite of all he has done and become, he is deeply loved. And in the knowledge of that love his heart expands with generosity toward others and Zacchaeus becomes a man, a person, of jubilee.

"Hurry and come down," Christ says to each one of us. Hurry and come down, come down out of your tree of unawareness and enter into the love with which I love you, which is your freedom and your joy. So Frank, Mary, Sharon, Pat, David, whoever you may be, hurry down, for I must stay in the house of your heart today.

How do you hear Christ's invitation to come down into a place of greater awareness in your life today? How have you been invited to "come down" out of places of singularity and aloofness and enter more deeply into the common life we share?

72

Love divine, all loves excelling,
    joy of heaven, to earth come down,
fix in us thy humble dwelling,
    all thy faithful mercies crown.
Jesus, thou art all compassion,
    pure, unbounded love thou art;
visit us with thy salvation,
    enter every trembling heart.

Come, almighty to deliver,
    let us all thy life receive;
suddenly return, and never,
    nevermore thy temples leave.
Thee we would be alway blessing,
    serve thee as thy hosts above,
pray, and praise thee without ceasing,
    glory in thy perfect love.

Finish then thy new creation;
    pure and spotless let us be;
let us see thy great salvation
    perfectly restored in thee:
changed from glory into glory,
    till in heaven we take our place,
till we cast our crowns before thee,
    lost in wonder, love, and praise.

Charles Wesley,
Hymn 657 in The Hymnal 1982

◊

nine

Go Forth in My Name

When Jesus saw the crowds, he went up the mountain; and after he sat down, his disciples came to him. Then he began to speak, and taught them, saying: "Blessed are the poor in spirit, for theirs is the kingdom of heaven. Blessed are those who mourn, for they will be comforted. Blessed are the meek, for they will inherit the earth. Blessed are those who hunger and thirst for righteousness, for they will be filled. Blessed are the merciful, for they will receive mercy. Blessed are the pure in heart, for they will see God. Blessed are the peacemakers, for they will be called children of God. Blessed are those who are persecuted for righteousness' sake, for theirs is the kingdom of heaven. Blessed are you when people revile you and persecute you and utter all kinds of evil against you falsely on my account. Rejoice and be glad, for your reward is great in heaven, for in the same way they persecuted the prophets who were before you."

Matthew 5:1-12

Jesus "went up the mountain; and after he sat down, his disciples came to him. Then he began to speak, and taught them, saying...." And what is it that he taught them? First of all, he taught them out of the deep interiority of his own life and prayer. He shared with the disciples the fruit of those times when he had headed into the hills to be alone with the one whom he addressed as "Abba, Father."

He taught them out of his temptations, his near despair over the seeming failure of his mission to move the hearts of his people. He taught them out of his frustration over his inability to crack his people open by the proclamation of the liberating of the Lord's favor. They were too defended, too caught up in the religious structures that claimed to mediate God's compassion while keeping God safely at bay.

He taught them out of his continuing struggle to remain faithful to the mystery of his own belovedness, a fidelity that required him over and over again to cry out as he did in Gethsemene on the eve of his crucifixion, "Abba, Father, for you all things are possible; remove this cup from me; yet, not what I want, but what you want" (Mark 14:36).

The beatitudes Jesus sets before his disciples represent an act of profound intimacy in which he hands over to those who have companioned him the secrets of his own heart. He does so not in the form of a command—do this, do that—but in the form of brief declarations, some of them quite paradoxical in that they can only reveal themselves as true as they are experienced and lived. Contrary to the way in which the beatitudes are frequently presented, their message is not always self-evident. They are elusive and make sense only to those who are available to the driving motion of the Spirit that blows where it wills in sovereign freedom, turning things upside down and inside out, including our tidy structures and well-ordered pieties.

In many of our parishes it has become a regular practice to renew our baptismal vows. In so doing we reaffirm our availability to God's project of reordering all relationships in the purifying fire of God's deathless love made known in Christ, who became for us wisdom from God, our righteousness and sanctification and redemption. The powerful words of the baptismal covenant defy easy explication, but suggest by their sheer force and weight something of the foundational relationship between Christ and ourselves that baptism celebrates and the renewal of our baptismal vows affirms. It is in Christ, who is "the power of God and the wisdom of God" (1 Corinthians 1:24), that we discover our true selves, not in some finished state but very much under construction, both personally and as a community of faith. And it is the baptismal covenant, with its dynamic of believing, or rather trusting, and then continuing, persevering, repenting, proclaiming, seeking, serving, and striving, that accomplishes within us, in God's own way and God's own time, what the eighteenth-century priest and mystic William Law called the "process of Christ."

The very terms of our mission, our particular function within the context of God's ongoing work of reconciliation—as limbs and members of Christ's body—draw us evermore deeply into the mystery of Christ, which is to discover who in grace and truth we are and are called to be. And therefore, occasions when we are asked to renew our baptismal vows and to assume particular responsibilities in the life of the church are not simply occasions for taking on tasks and duties, but are opportunities to open ourselves and declare our availability to the deepest dimensions of our own belovedness.

God's invitation to exercise ministry and service in any form is always an act of God's love and an invitation to grow in the awareness of who we are, not on our own terms but according to God's seemingly indiscriminate pleasure and delight. If God's will for us is a desire for our full flourishing, then every yielding to God's will is a gesture of possibility and blessing we extend to ourselves.

In baptism Christ offers us freedom: we are told "for freedom Christ has set us free" (Galatians 5:1). And yet that freedom does not stand on its own: it is the consequence, the fruit of our relationship to Christ. "If you continue in my word," says Christ—if you abide, if you remain, if you make your home in my word, which is my deep love for you—"you are truly my disciples; and you will know the truth, and the truth will make you free" (John 8:31-32). Christ, who calls us friends, not servants, invites us into intimate collaboration with him in doing the will of the One who sent him and accomplishing his work.

Christ, through the Spirit, gives us gifts, charisms, as manifestations of Christ's loving desire that we join him in the ongoing task of binding up, setting free, and making all things new. May each one of us receive these gifts with open and available hearts, ready to hear Christ the Risen One in whom we are set free say, "You are gifted with my grace, you are the light of the world. Now go forth in my name, proclaim jubilee, and above all, surprise me."

◊

Almighty God, we thank you that by the death and resurrection of your Son Jesus Christ you have overcome sin and brought us to yourself, and that by the sealing of your Holy Spirit you have bound us to your service. Renew is us your servants the covenant you made with us at our Baptism. Send us forth in the power of that Spirit to perform the service you set before us; through Jesus Christ your Son our Lord,

*who lives and reigns with you and the Holy
Spirit, one God, now and for ever. Amen*

*Prayer at the Reaffirmation
of Baptismal Vows, BCP 309*

Endnotes

1. Abraham Joshua Heschel, *The Sabbath* (New York: Farrar, Straus & Giroux, 1995), 29.
2. Gail Godwin, *Evensong* (New York: Ballantine, 1999).
3. Stephen Mitchell, ed., *The Enlightened Heart: An Anthology of Sacred Poetry* (New York: Harper Perennial, 1963).

DATE DUE

			Printed in USA